HEROES
OF THE US MILITARY

HEROES OF THE US AIR FORCE

By Barbara M. Linde

Gareth Stevens
Publishing

Please visit our website, www.garethstevens.com. For a free color catalog of all our high-quality books, call toll free 1-800-542-2595 or fax 1-877-542-2596.

Library of Congress Cataloging-in-Publication Data

Linde, Barbara M.
Heroes of the US Air Force / Barbara M. Linde.
    pages cm. — (Heroes of the US military)
Includes index.
ISBN 978-1-4339-7233-1 (pbk.)
ISBN 978-1-4339-7234-8 (6-pack)
ISBN 978-1-4339-7232-4 (library binding)
1. United States. Air Force—Juvenile literature. 2. Air pilots, Military—United States—Juvenile literature. I. Title.
UG633.L5 2012
358.40092'273—dc23

                          2011053508

First Edition

Published in 2013 by
Gareth Stevens Publishing
111 East 14th Street, Suite 349
New York, NY 10003

Copyright © 2013 Gareth Stevens Publishing

Designer: Michael J. Flynn
Editor: Therese Shea

Photo credits: Cover, p. 1 Tyler Stableford/Iconica/Getty Images; courtesy of US Air Force: pp. 4–5, 8–9, 12–13, 14, 16–17 by Tech Sgt. Justin D. Pyle, 18, 19 by Senior Airman Levi Riendeau, 23, 26 by Airman Leah Young, 27 by Staff Sgt. Eric Harris, 28–29 (F-22) by Senior Airman Gustavo Gonzalez, 29 (seal); p. 6 Hulton Archive/ Getty Images; p. 7 Science & Society Picture Library/Getty Images; pp. 10–11 Transcedental Graphics/ Archive Photos/Getty Images; p. 15 Photoquest/Archive Photos/Getty Images; pp. 20–21 NASA/ Archive Photos/Getty Images; pp. 24–25 David Huntley/Shutterstock.com.

Printed in the United States of America

CPSIA compliance information: Batch #CS12GS: For further information contact Gareth Stevens, New York, New York at 1-800-542-2595.

CONTENTS

Faster Than Sound 4

Early Air Force History .6

Air Force Decorations 10

Tuskegee Airmen 12

Flying Aces 14

Thunderbirds 16

Female Airmen 18

USAF Astronauts 20

Space and Cyberspace 22

Air Force One 24

A Skydiving Hero 26

"Aim High...Fly, Fight, Win" 28

Glossary 30

For More Information 31

Index 32

NOV 2012

Words in the glossary appear in **bold** type the first time they are used in the text

FASTER THAN SOUND

US Air Force test pilot Chuck Yeager changed flight forever on October 14, 1947. He took his plane to a speed of 700 miles (1,126 km) per hour, faster than the speed of sound! He was the first pilot to do this.

Chuck Yeager named his Bell X-1 plane "Glamorous Glennis" after his wife.

Yeager thought of himself as a **combat** pilot more than a test pilot. During World War II, Yeager shot down 13 enemy planes, five in one day. Later, he commanded **squadrons** and flew combat **missions** in Europe and Southeast Asia. Yeager also trained astronauts for the US space program. He remains one of the most famous of the many heroes of the US Air Force.

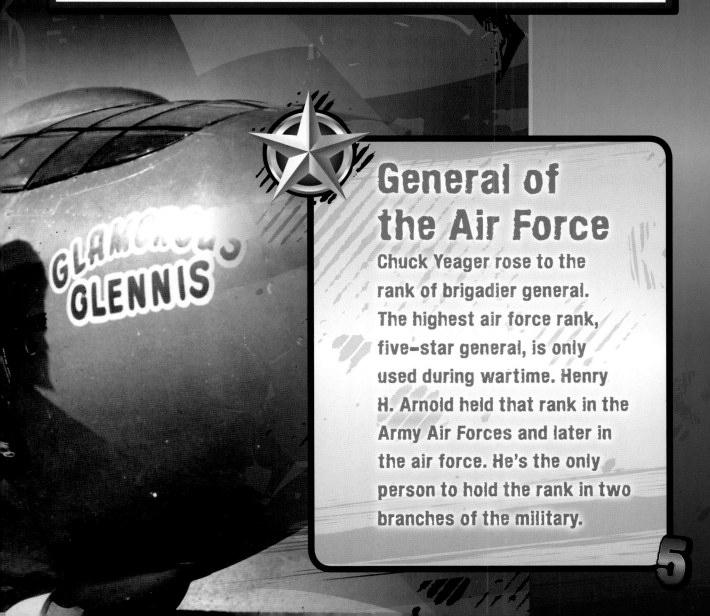

GLAMOROUS GLENNIS

General of the Air Force

Chuck Yeager rose to the rank of brigadier general. The highest air force rank, five-star general, is only used during wartime. Henry H. Arnold held that rank in the Army Air Forces and later in the air force. He's the only person to hold the rank in two branches of the military.

EARLY AIR FORCE HISTORY

In 1907, the US Army Signal **Corps** created a flight unit called the Aeronautical Division. It had three men and no airplanes. Captain Benjamin Foulois helped form the 1st Aero Squadron in 1913. He and his crew began trying out many kinds of airplanes. At that time, airplanes were still very new, so this was dangerous work.

Airplanes were used in war for the first time during World War I. Brigadier General William "Billy" Mitchell was in charge of several air squadrons sent overseas. He also worked hard to convince officials that airplanes had a future with the US military.

Brigadier General Mitchell, on the right, was a World War I leader and hero. The airport in Milwaukee, Wisconsin, is named for him.

This photo shows a Wright Flyer in 1908, a year before the army bought its first plane.

First Flight

On December 17, 1903, Wilbur and Orville Wright made history by successfully flying an engine-powered airplane. In 1909, the US Army bought its first airplane from the Wright brothers. However, even before this, flight had been a part of the military. During the American Civil War, hot-air balloons were used to spot enemy forces.

Established in 1941, the Army Air Forces helped win World War II with their 2.4 million members and 80,000 planes. The United States Air Force (USAF) split off from the army on September 18, 1947, and became a branch of the military equal to the army and navy.

Air Forces Day was established on August 1, 1946, by President Harry Truman (left).

Since then, the air force has pursued its mission to protect us in the air and in space. It has continuously updated its planes with cutting-edge **technology**. In recent years, the air force has added cyberspace, which includes the Internet and other means of electronic communication, to its areas of responsibility.

Air Force Academy

The United States Air Force Academy near Colorado Springs, Colorado, is both a military training base and a 4-year university. Students study math, science, and other subjects. They also learn to fly and prepare for careers as air force officers. The first class graduated in June 1959.

AIR FORCE DECORATIONS

As Army Air Captain Charles Lindberg's plane, *The Spirit of St. Louis*, landed near Paris, France, on May 21, 1927, onlookers clapped and cheered. Lindberg, or "Lucky Lindy," had just become the first person to fly alone and nonstop across the Atlantic Ocean. Because of this heroic action, he was awarded the Medal of Honor.

The Medal of Honor is the highest award an airman can receive. Lindberg's medal was rare, as it's usually given for heroism in combat with the enemy. The Air Force Cross is the next highest award. Other decorations honor achievements in flight, rifle skills, and good conduct.

Longest Service

Major General Alfred K. Flowers received the Distinguished Service Medal when he retired in early 2012. With 46 years of active duty, Flowers holds the record for the longest service in the air force. He had more than 25 assignments during that time. Before he retired, he was in charge of planning the air force's budget.

On his famous flight in 1927, Lindberg spent 33½ hours in the air, flying about 3,600 miles (5,790 km).

TUSKEGEE AIRMEN

In the mid-1900s, many parts of American life, including the military, were still **segregated**. In 1941, the Army Air Corps created an African American unit named the Tuskegee Airmen. Its members learned to fly and maintain aircraft. By 1945, nearly 1,000 men had completed pilot training.

The Tuskegee Airmen trained at Tuskegee Institute and Tuskegee Army Air Field in Alabama.

These airmen flew 1,500 missions in Europe and North Africa. They took down more than 400 German planes and sank a battleship destroyer. While many of these airmen received medals for bravery, about 150 died. The Tuskegee Airmen's 332nd Fighter Group earned an award for heroism. Their courage and skill helped end segregation in the military.

Two Generations

Master Sergeant Harvey Haynes, a Tuskegee Airman, was a member of a bomber crew during World War II. His granddaughter, Mareshah Haynes, later became an airman. Among other duties, Technical Sergeant Haynes writes articles and takes photographs for the official air force website.

FLYING ACES

An ace is a fighter pilot who shoots down five or more enemy aircraft. Records of famous aces have been kept since World War I.

Captain Edward Rickenbacker was the first known ace. He had 26 "aerial victories" in World War I. First Lieutenant Boyd Wagner, the first World War II Army Air Forces ace, shot down 8 planes. Major Richard Bong led the World War II aces with 40 victories. He's still the top ace of all time. Major James Jabara became the first USAF jet ace. He shot down 15 planes during the **Korean War**.

Major James Jabara, shown here, died in a car crash in 1966 before he could serve in Vietnam.

Francis Gabreski flew 266 combat missions in two wars.

Double Aces

A few pilots earned the title of ace in two wars. Colonel Francis Gabreski was the top ace for combined service in World War II (28) and the Korean War (6.5). (In some wars, credit was divided between pilots.) Colonel Robin Olds is the only ace from World War II (12) and the **Vietnam War** (4).

THUNDERBIRDS

Called "America's **Ambassadors** in Blue," the Thunderbirds have been exhibiting the air power and skill of the US Air Force since 1953. The Thunderbirds give 70 or more hour-long shows every year. Today, 12 officers pilot the F-16 Fighting Falcon jet fighters. More than 120 airmen serve as the support crew. It's thrilling to watch as the planes twirl, roll, and dive both solo and in formation.

Lieutenant Colonel Case Cunningham, the current commander, uses his experience of 2,400 flight hours and 160 hours in combat to guide his team. The Thunderbirds both represent and honor all airmen serving at home and overseas.

Origin of the Name

The official name of the Thunderbirds is the US Air Force Air Demonstration Unit. The original unit chose the nickname "Thunderbirds" after a Native American myth about a giant bird. The bird's flight made the earth tremble. Its wings made a sound like thunder—much like the F-16!

The Thunderbirds perform at air bases all over the world, including Australia, Japan, and Korea.

FEMALE AIRMEN

Congress has allowed women pilots to fly combat missions since 1991. These airmen may also be assigned to support units in war zones and on air force bases.

Lieutenant Colonel Merryl Tengesdal was the first African American woman to fly a U-2 **reconnaissance** plane. Captain Heather Fox also flies reconnaissance missions in a U-2. U-2s are planes that demand pilots of great skill and are among the hardest to land safely. They're flown at heights of 70,000 feet (21,336 m) above the ground. Both Tengesdal and Fox have carried important messages to and from American troops in Afghanistan and Iraq.

In 2004, Merryl Tengesdal left the navy to join the air force's U-2 program.

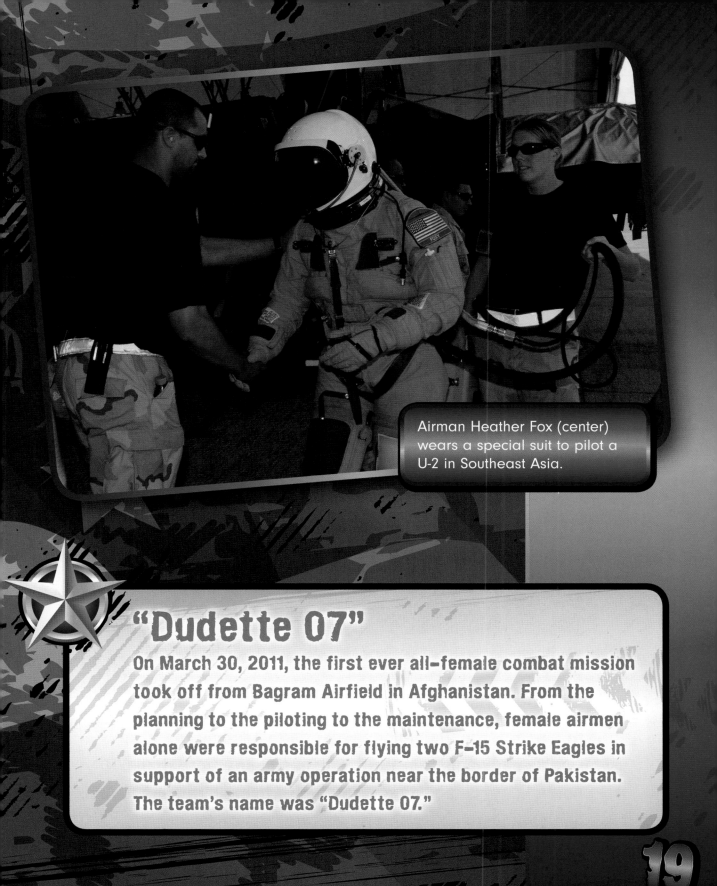

Airman Heather Fox (center) wears a special suit to pilot a U-2 in Southeast Asia.

"Dudette 07"

On March 30, 2011, the first ever all-female combat mission took off from Bagram Airfield in Afghanistan. From the planning to the piloting to the maintenance, female airmen alone were responsible for flying two F-15 Strike Eagles in support of an army operation near the border of Pakistan. The team's name was "Dudette 07."

USAF ASTRONAUTS

The NASA (National Aeronautics and Space Administration) astronaut program began in 1958. Since early astronauts were required to be jet pilots, many were also in the air force.

Lieutenant Colonel Virgil "Gus" Grissom was a fighter pilot who became one of the first Project Mercury astronauts. Project Mercury was the first US manned spaceflight program. Sadly, Grissom died in 1967 when a fire broke out on *Apollo 1*.

Two years later, USAF Colonel Buzz Aldrin piloted *Apollo 11* during the first manned lunar landing on July 20, 1969. Aldrin became the second person to walk on the moon.

Firsts in Space

In 1995, Colonel Eileen Collins became the first female pilot of a space shuttle. Collins went on to become the first female commander in 1999. She has spent more than 870 hours in space and over 6,750 hours flying airplanes. Collins has earned many NASA and air force awards.

Buzz Aldrin spent 2 hours and 15 minutes walking on the moon.

SPACE AND CYBERSPACE

The Air Force Space Command, established in 1982, uses many kinds of **satellites**. Some operate in wartime to exchange information between defense officials on and off the battlefield. Other satellites track space and man-made objects around Earth.

In recent years, defending the nation's computers and satellites from **terrorists** has become an important part of modern defense. Lieutenant General Robert Elder helped create the Air Force Cyber Command in 2006. More than 5,400 engineers, programmers, and other computer experts conduct 24-hour cyberspace operations, proving people can be heroes while sitting at a desk.

The Wild Blue Yonder

The official Air Force song starts with the words "Off we go into the wild blue yonder." Written by Robert Crawford, it was chosen in a contest and first performed in 1939. In 1971, the *Apollo 15* mission took a page of the song to the moon.

The air force's Atlas V is the current launch system of US military satellites.

AIR FORCE ONE

The name "Air Force One" is given to either of two special air force jets whenever the president is on board. USAF Colonel Mark Tillman was an Air Force One pilot for President George W. Bush. On September 11, 2001, terrorists attacked the World Trade Center in New York City. No one knew if the president and Air Force One were in danger, too.

UNITED STA

The term "Air Force One" applies to any air force jet on which the president of the United States is flying.

Tillman's goal was to keep the president safe. He requested fighter jets to protect the plane. He piloted Air Force One safely to an air force base in Louisiana. Tillman continued to pilot the jet for President Bush, traveling to 75 countries and 49 of the United States.

A Sad Duty

USAF Colonel James Swindal was President John F. Kennedy's personal pilot. He flew Air Force One to Dallas, Texas, on November 22, 1963. After Kennedy was killed later that day, Swindal had the sad duty of flying Kennedy's body back to Washington, DC. Colonel Swindal later said that he felt "that the world had ended."

A SKYDIVING HERO

Staff Sergeant Shaun Meadows joined the air force after the September 11 terrorist attacks. While fighting in Afghanistan in 2008, his truck ran over a bomb. Doctors saved his life, but he lost his legs. Back in the United States, Meadows was fitted with **artificial** legs and learned to walk again. He decided to return to the activities he had once enjoyed—such as skydiving!

After his historic jump, Sergeant Meadows said, "It felt good to get up there and jump again after 2 years."

On June 15, 2010, Meadows joined his squadron members in a jump. He made history as the first active duty double **amputee** airman to successfully complete a jump. His bravery is a model for other wounded warriors.

The Wounded Warrior Program organizes events such as bike rides in support of injured veterans.

Wounded Warriors

The Wounded Warrior Program helps airmen and other military who were injured during combat. They receive assistance whether they choose to stay in the air force or leave. Care managers help airmen make the change from military to civilian life. The program also sponsors social and athletic activities such as the Warrior Games.

"AIM HIGH . . . FLY, FIGHT, WIN"

The air force adopted a new **motto** in 2010. It combines the old motto, "Aim High," with the phrase "Fly, Fight, Win." The change was selected by the airmen themselves and reflects their total commitment to excel in service to their country.

An F-22 Raptor soars home to an air force base in Hawaii. The F-22 is the most advanced fighter jet to date.

The air force mission is "to fly, fight, and win . . . in air, space, and cyberspace." Every day, airmen live their motto and work tirelessly toward their mission. As the last line of the air force song says, "Nothing'll stop the US Air Force!" All airmen are heroes, on the ground and in the wild blue yonder.

The Air Force Seal

Each symbol on the official air force seal has a special meaning. Blue and gold are the air force colors. The 13 stars stand for the original 13 colonies. The bald eagle and thunderbolts represent air power. The year the air force was established, 1947, is shown in roman numerals.

GLOSSARY

ambassador: one who serves as an official representative for a group or country

amputee: someone who has had a limb removed

artificial: made by people rather than nature

combat: armed fighting between opposing forces. Also, to fight against someone or something.

corps: a group of soldiers trained for special service

Korean War: a conflict between North and South Korea that began in 1950 and ended in 1953 in which the United States joined with South Korea

mission: a task or job a group must perform

motto: a short saying that expresses a rule to live by

reconnaissance: the exploration of a place to collect information

satellite: an object that circles Earth in order to collect and send information or aid in communication

segregated: limited to members of one group or race

squadron: a division of military organization, smaller than a unit but larger than a platoon

technology: the study, making, and use of tools and machines

terrorist: someone who uses violence and fear to challenge an authority

Vietnam War: a conflict starting in 1955 and ending in 1975 between South Vietnam and North Vietnam in which the United States joined with South Vietnam

FOR MORE INFORMATION

Books

Camelo, Wilson. *The U.S. Air Force and Military Careers*. Berkeley Heights, NJ: Enslow Publishers, 2006.

Doeden, Matt. *The U.S. Air Force*. Mankato, MN: Capstone Press, 2009.

Websites

American Visionaries: Tuskegee Airmen
www.cr.nps.gov/museum/exhibits/tuskegee/airoverview.htm
Read about the history and achievements of the Tuskegee Airmen.

National Museum of the US Air Force
www.nationalmuseum.af.mil
View historic planes, uniforms, and other military items.

The Official Website of the US Air Force
www.af.mil
Learn the history of the air force, and read about current missions.

INDEX

Aeronautical Division 6

Air Force Cyber Command 22

Air Force One 24, 25

Air Force Space Command 22

Aldrin, Buzz 20, 21

Army Air Corps 12

Army Air Forces 5, 8, 14

Arnold, Henry H. 5

astronauts 5, 20

awards 10, 13, 20

Bong, Richard 14

Collins, Eileen 20

Cunningham, Case 16

"Dudette 07" 19

Elder, Robert 22

1st Aero Squadron 6

Flowers, Alfred K. 10

Foulois, Benjamin 6

Fox, Heather 18, 19

Gabreski, Francis 15

Grissom, Virgil "Gus" 20

Haynes, Harvey 13

Haynes, Mareshah 13

Jabara, James 14

Lindberg, Charles 10, 11

Meadows, Shaun 26, 27

Mitchell, William "Billy" 6

NASA 20

Olds, Robin 15

Rickenbacker, Edward 14

Swindal, James 25

Tengesdal, Merryl 18

Thunderbirds 16, 17

Tillman, Mark 24, 25

Tuskegee Airmen 12, 13

US Army Signal Corps 6

Wagner, Boyd 14

Wright, Wilbur and Orville 7

Yeager, Chuck 4, 5